NOTHING Is IMPOSSIBLE with God

WORKBOOK

Eleven Bible Heroes, One God, and Endless Lessons in Overcoming

SHANNON BREAM

HarperChristian Resources

Nothing Is Impossible with God Workbook

Published by HarperChristian Resources, 3950 Sparks Drive SE, Suite 101, Grand Rapids, MI 49546, USA.
HarperChristian Resources is a registered trademark of HarperCollins Christian Publishing, Inc.

Requests for information should be addressed to customercare@harpercollins.com.

ISBN 978-0-310-18562-8 (softcover)
ISBN 978-0-310-18563-5 (ebook)

HarperChristian Resources titles may be purchased in bulk for church, business, fundraising, or ministry use. For information, please email ResourceSpecialist@ChurchSource.com.

HarperCollins Publishers, Macken House, 39/40 Mayor Street Upper, Dublin 1, D01 C9W8, Ireland (https://www.harpercollins.com).

Art Direction: Ron Huizinga
Cover Design: Caroline Johnson
Interior Design: Lauren Curfman

First Printing May 2026 / Printed in the United States of America

Contents

Welcome

Years ago, I struggled with a chronic condition that left me in excruciating pain—the kind that ranks ten out of ten. I visited a long list of doctors in search of a diagnosis. Months bled into years as I suffered. I grew increasingly despondent and depressed.

I prayed, "God, if it's not Your will to heal me, will You please lead me to the right medical professional who can help me?"

I eventually discovered a doctor who diagnosed me with map-dot-fingerprint dystrophy. This genetic condition caused the surface of my corneas to tear repeatedly. When the doctor said he knew how to help me, my heart flooded with hope and joy.

Then he said the words I never wanted to hear:

"There's no cure."

I retreated to my car and wept, eyes swollen with grief. I couldn't imagine living with this pain for the rest of my life. I begged God to help, to heal, to do anything.

That's when the Lord whispered in my Spirit, *I will be with you.*

He didn't promise I'd be healed or that everything would suddenly be okay. He simply assured me of one thing: He would walk with me through whatever came. And that promise has been enough—sustaining me through different medications and eventually a surgery that brought an end to nearly all the physical and emotional suffering the disease had caused.

I share that because, like me, maybe you've encountered situations where it feels impossible—where you want or need to overcome something and you just can't. Maybe right now life feels like too much. You don't see a way forward. And God feels a million miles away. If that's you, I get you, and you are not alone.

There's a long list of biblical heroes who have felt the same way. They've wandered and wondered. They've struggled and suffered. They've felt disappointment and defeat. And yet they've overcome simply because God was with them.

In the upcoming pages, we'll explore the stories of eleven people from the Bible and the impossible situations they faced. These individuals wrestled with the same issues we do—everything from imposter syndrome to social anxiety to paralyzing fear to significant trauma. They dealt with the same feelings we do, too—those of loneliness, rejection, and being overwhelmed. They faced impossible odds, yet they overcame because God was with them. And with God, you can overcome too.

How to Use This Workbook

This workbook is a companion to the *New York Times* bestselling book *Nothing Is Impossible with God* by Shannon Bream, and it's designed to make your experience richer and deeper. In the upcoming eleven lessons, you'll be challenged to consider the parallels between each person's story and your own. You'll be asked to reflect on how God worked in their lives and how He's working in your own life.

If you join with friends or neighbors to complete this workbook, consider answering the questions personally *before* you meet up. That way you'll be prepared with insights, reflections, and thoughts to share.

You'll notice that each lesson has four components:

REFLECT invites you to read key moments of each person's life in the Bible and connect with their story.

CONNECT asks you to consider how God in the Old Testament or Jesus in the New Testament responds to each person and what this discloses about His character and how He responds to you.

REVEAL provides an opportunity to identify specific character traits, responses to God, and acts of faith, as well as your similar traits, responses, and acts of faith.

PRAY asks you to prayerfully consider how the person's story ties into the work God is doing in your life right now.

LESSON ONE

Gideon's Imposter Syndrome

Ultimately, your inadequacies (perceived or real) are never a limit on God's ability to equip you for the task He's assigned you to. . . . Gideon's story is an authentic illustration for us of how relying on God can give us true freedom from fear.

SHANNON BREAM

from *Nothing Is Impossible with God*

In exploring the Bible, it's easy to imagine we'll find confident, flawless, perfect people with well-honed skills and heroic courage. Yet more often, we find everyday people just like you and me—men and women filled with questions and doubts and weaknesses who often second-guess what God is calling them to do.

If you've ever wrestled with self-doubt or felt that you're ill-equipped to do what God has called you to do, you'll find hope and encouragement in the life of Gideon. He battled with something known as imposter syndrome. It's the deep feeling that you're not as competent as others perceive you to be. It's the nagging sense that you'll be found out as a fraud or that you don't have what it takes to do the task before you.

Gideon's story reminds us that God doesn't just call the qualified; He qualifies the called. And wobbly self-reliance can become sturdy God-reliance whenever we respond in obedience.

Reflect

Gideon's story appears in the book of Judges, which recounts a period in Israel's history before its first king. During this time, Israel repeated a pattern so often that it became a predictable, recurring cycle. The nation would do evil, fall under the judgment of God, and would be rescued by a God-appointed judge. When Gideon first appears in Judges 6, the Lord has given Israel into the hands of the Midianites.

Read Judges 6:1–6. How did the Israelites suffer and become disheartened under the Midianites?

What recent situation has been discouraging to you?

Which element of your situation caused you to ask the Lord for help?

How have you sensed the Lord respond?

In response to the Israelites' cry for help, the Lord appoints a prophet who reminds the Israelites what got them into this situation.

Read Judges 6:7–10. What does the prophet remind the Israelites?

When Gideon first appears in the Bible, he's threshing wheat—the process of separating the grain from the rest of the plant after harvest. Gideon is hiding in a winepress to protect the valuable food source from the Midianites.

Read Judges 6:11–12. How does the Holy Messenger greet Gideon?

Take a moment and imagine the Holy Messenger appearing and speaking these words to you. Which of the following best describes how you would feel if the Holy Messenger greeted you in this way? Circle all that apply.

Excited	Angry	Joyful	Confused	Anxious	Hopeful
Fearful	Irked	Sorrowful	Leery	Eager	Worried

Reflecting on the Messenger's words in Judges 6:12, which part of the greeting is easiest to accept for yourself? Which is hardest? Why?

Instead of celebrating the arrival of this divine message—and Messenger—Gideon launches into a cross-examination.

Read Judges 6:13–14. What concerns does Gideon raise in response to the divine message and Messenger?

What does Gideon's response reveal about his frustrations with God?

Which of the following best describes the divine Messenger's response to Gideon in verse 14? Circle all that apply.

Empowering	Critical	Action-oriented	Confident
Disappointed	Unmoved	Affirming	Commanding

Read Judges 6:15. How does Gideon wrestle with *imposter syndrome*—the idea that he doesn't have what it takes to do what God has called him to do?

What specific situations, environments, or types of achievements tend to trigger in you the feeling of being an imposter?

What nagging feeling or thought spiral tries to tell you that you can't do what you're called, appointed, or positioned by God to do in this stage of life?

What you have—plus what the Lord brings to the battle—
will always be enough.

Read Judges 6:16. How does the Lord respond to Gideon's imposter syndrome and self-doubt?

In what area of your life do you most need to hear the Lord say, "I will be with you"?

Gideon wants assurance that this incredible offer from the Lord is true. So he goes inside to prepare a meal, a precious offering for the divine Messenger.

Read Judges 6:17–24. What finally convinces Gideon that this is the Lord?

God gives Gideon his first mission, and it's not an easy one. Gideon must tear down his dad's altar to Baal, a pagan god, along with its accompanying Asherah pole—a wooden object or tree dedicated to the Canaanite fertility goddess Asherah.

Gideon must destroy these symbols of the people's sin—the gods they pray to for protection—and build a new altar with a proper sacrifice. Gideon knows his actions will be seen as treasonous and reckless, so rather than go midday, he takes ten servants and performs the task in the middle of the night.

Read Judges 6:25–31. How do Gideon's neighbors respond to his obedience to God?

What argument does Gideon's father, Joash, use to save his son (verse 31)?

Led by the Spirit, Gideon receives a second task: Assemble an army. Soon, thirty-two thousand men answer the call to go into battle. Yet self-doubt and imposter syndrome still plague Gideon. Not wanting to fail or look foolish, he asks God for confirmation not just once, but twice.

Read Judges 6:36–40. What does Gideon ask of God, and how does God respond?

What does God's response to Gideon reveal about the times we ask Him for assurance?

How does this encourage you?

Much like us, Gideon is on a journey of growing in God-reliance and faith.

Read Judges 7:2–8. How does the reduction of troops strip Gideon of self-reliance or any perception of strength?

Just as God knows our every hesitation and concern, God knows Gideon's too. In His love, God addresses Gideon's fears before he can even say them aloud.

Read Judges 7:9–11. How does the Lord help Gideon overcome his fears?

Just as Gideon arrives in the enemy's camp, he hears a soldier telling a friend about a dream: A round loaf of barley bread came tumbling into the Midianite camp and struck the tent with such force that it collapsed.

Read Judges 7:14–15. How is the dream interpreted by the other soldier? How does Gideon respond?

God knows we may be faint of heart, but He doesn't leave us there. Gideon's story reminds us that God can use us even when we doubt, hesitate, and second-guess ourselves. With every faith-filled step forward, we move toward overcoming—both our fears and the odds stacked against us.

Read Judges 7:16–25. What does Gideon instruct his army to do, and what is the outcome?

Gideon's unusual instructions to his soldiers require them to act in faith. The blast of hundreds of trumpets, followed by the crash of the jars, followed by the blazing torches illuminating the skies convince the Midianites that a much larger force is attacking. The Midianites run away, crying aloud as they flee. God makes the impossible possible.

Much like their demand for a king at the end of the book of Judges, the Israelites direct their adoration toward a human source—Gideon—rather than God Himself.

Read Judges 8:22–24. What do the people ask of Gideon, and how does he respond?

Gideon's request for a share of the plunder eventually becomes a snare to Gideon, his family, and God's people. Yet for the remainder of Gideon's life, peace reigns in the land (verse 28). The adventures of Gideon remind us that the antidote to imposter syndrome and all those pesky self-doubts is wholehearted reliance on God.

On the continuum below, mark how much you struggle with imposter syndrome—the nagging feeling that you don't have what it takes to do the task God has placed before you.

I find it easy to believe I can do what God has called me to do. —○—○—○—○—○—○—○— I find it hard to believe I have what it takes to do what God has called me to do.

In the space below, write a prayer asking God to remove any thoughts or feelings you have of being an imposter and reveal who He is in and through you.

Connect

Now that you've read and reflected on much of Gideon's story, it's time to connect this person of the Bible with your own life. Fill out the chart below.

What does Gideon's story teach you about overcoming imposter syndrome or feeling like a fraud?	
What challenges or encourages you most in Gideon's story?	
What does Gideon's story reveal about overcoming impossible situations?	
What is one area in which you hope to walk in greater confidence in God after studying Gideon's life?	

Reveal

Now that you've connected Gideon's story with your own life, it's time to look at how God reveals His character and faithfulness to Gideon and how God is doing the same for you.

Where do you see God show up in Gideon's life, and what does that reveal about God?	
What does God reveal to you about His character and faithfulness through the life of Gideon?	
What does Gideon's story suggest or reveal about the way God wants to empower you?	

Pray

Take a few minutes to ask the Holy Spirit to guide you as you respond to the following prayer prompts.

Lord, like Gideon, help me . . .

Lord, where am I doubting and second-guessing what You've called me to do in this season? What's the next step I need to take in obedience to You?

Lord, where am I most tempted not to trust You to do what You say You want to do through me? How can I trust You more?

Lord, considering Gideon's story, how are You calling me to live differently?

LESSON TWO

Moses's Social Anxiety

After 430 years of captivity, the people of Israel were delivered under the leadership of a man who would rather have hidden out with the sheep.

SHANNON BREAM
from *Nothing Is Impossible with God*

Have you ever felt a wave of social anxiety? Perhaps you've sensed it when you walk into a party and realize you don't know anyone there. The thought of starting up a series of conversations with strangers feels awkward or exhausting.

Or maybe you've felt it when you've had to speak up in a classroom or deliver a formal presentation. Being the center of attention may cause your heart to race. Or perhaps you've felt a wave of anxiety when you've had to call a stranger without the benefit of a script or seeing the person you're responding to.

Many of us have struggled with social anxiety. It's more than just shyness, occasional nervousness, or the fear of saying the wrong thing. It's rooted in how we believe others perceive us—an intense fear of being judged, embarrassed, or humiliated in vulnerable situations.

If you've ever wrestled with anxiety in a social situation, then you'll draw comfort and confidence from the life of Moses. He struggled with speaking up in public, yet God used him to overcome what seemed like an impossible situation: the Israelites' four-hundred-plus-year enslavement in Egypt.

Reflect

Moses's mother, Jochebed, is a wildly courageous woman. She refuses (along with other midwives) to obey the Egyptian pharaoh's edict that every Hebrew male baby must be killed. Instead, Jochebed hides baby Moses for three months. Then she crafts a floating basket, puts Moses in it, and places it among the reeds in the Nile.

Under the watchful eye of Moses's older sister, Miriam, Pharaoh's daughter discovers the basket and has compassion on baby Moses. In a string of "only God" events, Jochebed gets to nurse her own baby before delivering her boy to the palace to become the pharaoh's daughter's son.

Yet Moses never loses his link to his people. Later in his life, when he sees an Egyptian beating a Hebrew, he kills the Egyptian and buries him in the sand. When the secret of Moses's killing gets out, he flees for his life from Pharaoh. From a prince, Moses becomes a lowly shepherd living in the desert. Yet behind the scenes, God is positioning Moses for His purposes.

Read Exodus 2:23–25. Reflect on the following actions, writing what God hears, remembers, sees, and knows.

- HEAR:

- REMEMBER:

- SEE:

- KNOW:

What do your answers reveal about how God responds to suffering?

How does this comfort you in your own season of pain, loss, or grief?

While tending the flock of his father-in-law, Jethro, Moses sees a bush that is on fire and yet not consumed by the flame. Curious, he goes over to inspect the strange sight and has an unforgettable encounter with God.

Read Exodus 3:4–10. What does God's conversation with Moses reveal about how God accomplishes His purposes?

Read Exodus 3:11. Describe a situation in which you've found yourself identifying with Moses's response of "Who am I?"

How did God show Himself as faithful to you through that situation?

Read Exodus 3:12. How does God respond to Moses's concern?

Even after his fatal choice made him a man on the run, Moses was still being prepared for the critical assignment the Lord had already scripted for him.

Both Gideon and Moses receive God's promise, "I will be with you." Yet even with this divine guarantee, they both struggle with the task before them. Moses, in particular, has a laundry list of reasons why he can't do what God is asking.

Read Exodus 3:13–18. How does God address Moses's concern that the Israelites will not listen to him?

Moses needs reassurance. God has Moses drop his staff, which transforms into a snake and then back into a staff when Moses picks it up. Next, Moses tucks his hand into his cloak and pulls it out covered in disease—then tucks it back in, and his hand is healed. If those two miracles still don't convince Pharaoh, God tells Moses to pour water from the Nile on the ground and watch it turn to blood. Despite these miracles and instructions, Moses's fear of speaking up remains.

Read Exodus 4:10. What concern does Moses express?

Read Exodus 4:11–12. What does God remind Moses of?

How does Moses try to tell God no?

Describe a time when you argued with God. What was the outcome?

Describe a time when you told God no. What was the outcome?

In response, Exodus 4:14 tells us, "the LORD's anger burned against Moses." But God didn't give up on Moses, and thank goodness He never gives up on us! In His loving-kindness, God agrees to bring Moses's brother, Aaron, onto the team. Moses is instructed to give Aaron the words to say, and the Lord will speak through them.

Read Exodus 5:1–21. How does Pharaoh respond to Moses and Aaron's request?

How does the confrontation in verse 21 show that Moses's worst fears about approaching Pharaoh are coming true?

Read Exodus 5:22–23. What blunt concern does Moses bring before God? Do you think it's a fair concern? Why or why not?

Read Exodus 6:1–8. What is God's response to Moses?

What promises does God remind Moses of?

What role do the promises of God play in your life during difficult seasons or impossible situations?

Read Exodus 6:9–12. What deafened the Israelites from hearing God's instructions through Moses?

What tends to deafen you from hearing and responding to God's instruction and prompting?

Who do you think Moses was more afraid to speak to at this point: the Israelites or Pharaoh? Why?

How do Moses's self-doubt and fear regarding his speech surface again in verse 12?

Despite all the fear, anxiety, and rejection, Moses and Aaron remain faithful. Time and again, Pharaoh refuses to allow the Israelites to go, and each time another devastating plague is unleashed by God:

1. *Water turned to blood*
2. *Infestations of frogs*
3. *Infestations of gnats*
4. *Infestations of flies*
5. *Death of livestock*
6. *Painful boils*
7. *Hail*
8. *Swarms of locusts*
9. *Suffocating darkness*
10. *Death of the firstborn*

Amid the final plague of death, the Passover comes to life. God provides a way for His people to be shielded against the final judgment on Egypt. By spreading the blood of a sacrificed spotless lamb over their doorframes, the Israelites are saved. Passover illustrates the salvation that would come through the ultimate sacrificial lamb: Jesus Christ.

Following the devastation of the final plague, Pharaoh finally allows God's people to go free. They leave with the bounty of the land. But just as the Israelites begin to breathe a sigh of relief, Pharaoh changes his mind (again). God's people find themselves pinned up against the Red Sea with the Egyptian army chasing them down. The Israelites complain to Moses. Yet Moses is not the same as when we first met him.

Read Exodus 14:13–14. How does Moses's answer demonstrate that he has overcome insecurity and social anxiety in responding to God's people?

In what specific area is God calling you to do the following?

- DON'T BE AFRAID:

- STAND FIRM:

- SEE HIS DELIVERANCE:

- LET HIM FIGHT FOR YOU:

- BE STILL:

Reflecting on these five statements, which one comes easiest for you? Which is the hardest? Why?

How do these five statements empower you to overcome when anxiety stirs within you?

Moses reminds us that our anxieties, fears, and hesitations are no match for God. Just as God used Moses to set His people free, God wants to use you to help introduce others to His freedom, redemption, and the hope found in Christ. God doesn't call us despite our weaknesses; He calls us fully knowing our weaknesses yet knowing they do not define us—He alone does.

On the continuum below, mark how much you struggle with anxiety in social situations, speaking up, or presenting in public.

I find it easy to speak publicly and thrive in all social situations. ○—○—○—○—○—○—○ **I find it hard to speak publicly and thrive in all social situations.**

In the space below, write a prayer asking God to give you the strength and courage to navigate social situations, speak up, and even present in public with grace and confidence.

Connect

Now that you've read and reflected on much of Moses's story, it's time to connect this person of the Bible with your own life. Fill out the chart below.

What does Moses's story teach you about speaking up and overcoming social anxiety?	
What challenges or encourages you most in Moses's story?	
What does Moses's story reveal about overcoming impossible situations?	
How do you hope to walk in greater confidence in God after studying Moses's life?	

Reveal

Now that you've connected Moses's story with your own life, it's time to look at how God reveals His character and faithfulness to Moses and how God is doing the same for you.

Where do you see God show up in Moses's life, and what does that reveal about God?	
What does God reveal to you about His character and faithfulness through the life of Moses?	
What does Moses's story suggest or reveal about the way God wants to use you?	

Pray

Take a few minutes to ask the Holy Spirit to guide you as you respond to the following prayer prompts.

Lord, like Moses, help me . . .

Lord, where are You calling me to speak up or give a voice to the voiceless? What's the next step I need to take in obedience to You?

Lord, where am I hesitating or even hiding from what You want to do or say or accomplish through me? How can I respond to You in quicker obedience?

Lord, considering Moses's story, how are You calling me to live differently?

LESSON THREE

Peter's Fear

Bold and brash, fiery and unbridled—if you know much about Peter, that's probably your first impression of him. And you're not wrong. He spoke his mind, felt deeply, and acted quickly. . . . But the beauty in Peter's story, and ours, is that none of this ever meant he couldn't be redeemed and used by the Lord.

SHANNON BREAM

from *Nothing Is Impossible with God*

Like many of us, Peter wrestled with his faith—sometimes spectacularly. Impulsive and reactive, Peter often responded out of fear and insecurity. Yet none of this deterred the Son of God from using him. Despite Peter's failures, he was always part of God's bigger plan. The same grace that covered and restored Peter is available to us today.

Reflect

One of the most wondrous facets of Jesus is that He sees things in us that we cannot see in ourselves. When Andrew, a follower of John the Baptist, encounters Jesus, he races to tell his brother Simon. The Messiah has been found! Jesus greets Simon in a beautiful and intentional way.

Read John 1:40–42. Jesus uses the phrases "you are" and "you will be called." What is the meaning of the name Jesus gives Simon? (You may need to look this up in your Bible or online.) How is that meaning significant?

What is the meaning of your name? If you don't know, do a quick online search of your name's meaning.

Do you recognize any spiritual significance to the meaning of your name? If so, write about it below.

The gospels of Matthew, Mark, and Luke inform us that Jesus' formal call of Andrew and Peter took place on the shores of the Sea of Galilee. The fishermen brothers leave everything to follow Jesus and find themselves as front-row witnesses to the impossible.

Following the miraculous feeding of more than five thousand people on a hillside, Jesus tells His twelve disciples to go ahead of Him by boat to cross the Sea of Galilee. A storm soon mounts. Surrounded by whipping winds and crashing waves, Jesus appears near their small wooden vessel walking on the water.

Read Matthew 14:26–32. How does Peter's response to Jesus demonstrate great faith? How does Peter's response to the storm demonstrate great fear?

How does Jesus respond to the sinking of Peter, "the rock"?

What does this reveal about how Christ responds to us when our faith falters?

Verse 32 notes that the wind stops once Jesus and Peter are together back in the boat.

How have you experienced Jesus' presence transforming your storms?

Peter becomes a member of a trio, along with James and John, that Jesus keeps closest to Him. Together, they watch Jesus raise the daughter of Jairus, a religious leader, from the dead (Mark 5:37–42). It's moments like this that help Peter rightly identify Christ as the Messiah.

Read Matthew 16:13–17. What does Jesus affirm and promise Peter?

Despite Peter's bold declaration, he still struggles with what Jesus is teaching and revealing about His future.

Read Matthew 16:21–23. What does Peter misunderstand about Jesus' mission?

Jesus knows the brutal suffering before Him, but Peter adamantly resists embracing anything that could diminish Jesus as he already knows Him. In some ways, Peter places Jesus in a box—a box of protection and preservation. Anything that challenges Peter's understanding of who Jesus is, what Jesus will endure, and how Jesus should respond often spark fear and an extreme reaction from Peter. This is evident when Jesus washes the disciples' feet.

Read John 13:3–9. What does Peter initially refuse to allow Jesus to do?

How does Peter's response swing to the opposite extreme after Jesus' explanation?

At that same dinner, Jesus does something His devoted, intense follower finds even more shocking than the foot washing: He predicts that Peter's fear will get the best of him. Peter will soon deny multiple times that he even knows Jesus.

Read Matthew 26:33–35. What definitive promise does Peter make to Jesus?

Let's take a moment to reflect on the definitive word "never" that Peter often uses. It's the kind of absolute language that implies a situation in which there's never an exception.

"Never, Lord!" he said. "This shall never happen to you!" Matthew 16:22

"No," said Peter, "you shall never wash my feet." John 13:8

"I will never disown you." Matthew 26:35

When are you most likely to use definitive language such as "always" or "never"?

How can using less definitive statements lead to better relational outcomes?

> Jesus knows exactly how each of us will fail, and yet . . . He stands by, ready to envelop us in His loving arms when we return.

Peter does what he says he will "never" do. Yet Jesus' response to Peter reveals that none of us is beyond His redemption and restoration.

Read Luke 22:32. How does Jesus' response to Peter demonstrate prayerfulness and compassion?

Describe a time when you had both great faith and great fear. What was the outcome?

Before Peter denies knowing Christ, he first fails to be a faithful friend to Him. The Messiah asks His closest disciples to do one thing in the gut-wrenching hours leading up to His arrest, torture, and death.

Read Matthew 26:40–41. How do Peter and the other two disciples let Jesus down in His time of need?

On this long, dark night, Peter is on a fast track from failure to failure. When Judas, who has arranged to betray Jesus, shows up with Roman soldiers and Jewish religious leaders carrying torches and weapons, Jesus willingly submits. But Peter, operating out of fear, reaches for a sword.

Read John 18:10–11 and Luke 22:51. How does Jesus' response to Peter's action challenge Peter's understanding of the Messiah?

Then, in all four of the gospels, we see Peter doing the very thing he passionately promised he never would. Fear leads him to respond in complete and utter self-protection mode.

Read Mark 14:66–72. What does Peter feel in the wake of these denials?

Before Peter can become a leader in the early church, he experiences the devastating loss of Jesus and a deeper understanding of why Jesus came to earth. After the resurrection, Jesus doesn't just appear to Peter; Jesus pursues Peter.

Just as they were when Jesus first called them, Peter and Andrew are fishing in the Sea of Galilee. The resurrected Jesus, unrecognized by the men, stands on the shore and instructs them to put their nets on the right side of the boat. Fish flood the nets. And Peter reacts, well, quite Peter-ly, and jumps into the water to race to shore (John 21: 4–7).

After breakfast, Jesus addresses Peter.

Read John 21:15–17. Peter has denied Jesus three times, and now Peter makes three statements to Jesus. What are they?

1

2

3

Through Christ, Peter sheds his fear for love and finds his true purpose. Now Peter can channel his deep devotion to Jesus into building the early church. He no longer needs to live by the sword in his words or actions. Peter's story reminds us that Jesus wants to transform our fears into greater faith. And no matter how much you and I may feel like we have failed, God is waiting to renew us, rescue us, and redeem us for His glory.

On the continuum below, mark how much fear influences your responses and actions in your everyday life.

I find fear shaping many of my responses and actions. ○ ○ ○ ○ ○ ○ ○ I find fear doesn't affect any of my responses or actions.

In the space below, write a prayer asking God to give you the strength and courage to overcome your fears through His Spirit and step into His true purpose for you.

Connect

Now that you've read and reflected on much of Peter's story, it's time to connect this person of the Bible with your own life. Fill out the chart below.

What does Peter's story teach you about fear and how it can impact your words and actions?	
What challenges or encourages you most in Peter's story?	
What does Peter's story reveal about overcoming impossible situations?	
How do you hope to walk in greater faith in God after studying the life of Peter?	

Reveal

Now that you've connected Peter's story with your own life, it's time to look at how God reveals His character and faithfulness to Peter and how God is doing the same for you.

Where do you see Jesus show up in Peter's life, and what does that reveal about Him?	
What does Jesus reveal to you about His character and faithfulness through the life of Peter?	
What does Peter's story suggest or reveal about the way Jesus wants to heal and restore you?	

Pray

Take a few minutes to ask the Holy Spirit to guide you as you respond to the following prayer prompts.

Lord, like Peter, help me . . .

Lord, how am I allowing fear to get the best of me right now? What's the next step I need to take to trust You more?

Lord, where am I most tempted to deny Your power and presence in my life?

Lord, considering Peter's story, how are You calling me to live differently?

LESSON FOUR

Joseph's Family Trauma

If you've been betrayed in any way, you've gotten a taste of Joseph's early life. . . . The truly miraculous part of Joseph's story is not that he survived betrayal and suffering but that he didn't let it poison his faith in God and honorable view of authority. Instead of becoming bitter, Joseph trusted God and overcame the unfaithfulness of others—modeling what true fatherhood, brotherhood, and leadership look like.

SHANNON BREAM

from *Nothing Is Impossible with God*

Like me, I bet you've walked through situations and seasons that have left you confused, discouraged, and even angry. Maybe you were grasping for stability, and it felt like the floor dropped out from under you. Or perhaps you were in the process of rebuilding your life and midway through another storm toppled things again.

We wouldn't be human if we didn't wonder where God was and what He was doing in those moments. On this side of heaven, we don't always get the answers or clarity we desire. But every now and then, God graciously grants us understanding of what first appeared to be a series of unexplainable events.

This is particularly true of Joseph. Time and time again, the institutions, including family, friends, and the law, that should have protected Joseph . . . didn't. Yet Joseph's life reminds us that even when everything and everyone around us lets us down, God is still working behind the scenes to lift us up to where He intended all along.

Reflect

The beginning and end of Joseph's story are beautiful bookends, but the years in between are marked by betrayal, false accusations, and suffering. Often, just when things seem to be turning in Joseph's favor, he's blindsided by another heart-wrenching disappointment. Yet through it all, Joseph remains faithful to God even when others are unfaithful to him.

When we first meet Joseph, the son of Jacob, he's the favorite son of the favorite wife—the golden boy of the family.

Read Genesis 37:3–4. How does Jacob show favoritism to Joseph?

How do Joseph's brothers respond to their father's favoritism of Joseph?

When have you seen or experienced the harm that favoritism can cause in a family or workplace?

Joseph is treated with the honor of the firstborn even though he's a younger brother. Joseph's relationship with his brothers may have been redeemable if Joseph had responded with more humility and discretion, but alas, Joseph doesn't make things better for himself. Joseph acts as a tattletale and delivers a bad report about his brothers to his father. He even tells his brothers about his nighttime dreams that tout his superiority.

Read Genesis 37:5–11. How does Joseph's decision to share his dreams with his brothers further damage their already strained relationship?

Describe a time when you said something that you later wished you could take back. What was the outcome?

One day, Jacob sends Joseph on a sixty-plus-mile trek to his brothers to report back. When the brothers see Joseph, they stew with anger. They have finally had enough.

Read Genesis 37:18–35. Who and what stops Joseph's brothers from killing him?

How do Jacob's sons trick their own father?

How does Jacob respond to the news of the death of his favorite son?

The Midianites sell Joseph as a slave to Potiphar, one of Pharaoh's officers. Because "the LORD was with Joseph" (Genesis 39:2), Joseph becomes so trusted by Potiphar that he is placed in charge of everything Potiphar owns. God's favor rests on the entire household.

Potiphar's wife notices Joseph's attractiveness (verse 6) and tries to seduce him. But each time, Joseph refuses her advances.

Read Genesis 39:8–9. How does Joseph honor both his earthly master and his heavenly One?

Potiphar's wife doesn't take the rejection well. She lies and claims Joseph attacked her. Just as Joseph's brothers had abused their power by lying and betraying him, Potiphar's wife now does the same thing. Once again, Joseph is thrown into a dark hole. Instead of a well, this time it's an actual prison. And once again, God reveals that He is with Joseph.

Read Genesis 39:21–23. How does the Lord show favor to Joseph?

Eventually the Pharaoh's chief cupbearer and top baker join Joseph in prison. Both men have troubling dreams. Joseph offers to interpret their dreams and points to God as the divine source of information. He delivers good news to the cupbearer: He'll be restored to his position. But the baker receives grim news: His death is only days away.

Read Genesis 40:14, 20–23. What does Joseph ask the cupbearer to do, and how does the cupbearer respond?

Joseph spends two more years in prison waiting for something to change. Then, suddenly, something dramatic happens. Pharaoh has a pair of troubling dreams. He calls on every wise man and magician in Egypt for an interpretation, but no one can provide one. That's when the cupbearer remembers Joseph and his ability to interpret dreams. Pharaoh soon calls for Joseph.

Read Genesis 41:15–16. How does Joseph point to God rather than himself when responding to Pharaoh?

Joseph delivers the news that Egypt will experience seven years of plenty followed by seven years of famine. Joseph proposes a specific plan on how to make it through the difficult years.

Read Genesis 41:33–36. What is Joseph's plan?

Read Genesis 41:38–44. How does Pharaoh's response elevate Joseph and acknowledge God?

Everything comes true from Joseph's interpretation of Pharaoh's dreams. After the seven years of bounty, the seven years of famine follow. People from all over the world travel to Egypt for food—including Joseph's own brothers. Jacob sends ten of Joseph's brothers to Egypt for grain and keeps the youngest brother, Benjamin, at home.

Read Genesis 42:5–6. How are the dreams (Genesis 37:6–7, 9) that nearly got Joseph killed decades earlier finally coming true?

Joseph's brothers don't recognize him. He accuses them of being spies and interrogates them. That's how Joseph learns that his father, Jacob, is still alive, along with his youngest brother, Benjamin.

Under a false guise, the brothers who once cast Joseph into the darkness of a pit now find themselves cast into the darkness of a prison. Three days later, Joseph releases them and proposes a deal. If they want to prove they aren't spies, they must return with their youngest brother, Benjamin. To guarantee they follow through, Joseph keeps one brother, Simeon, behind as collateral.

Read Genesis 42:21–24. How does Joseph react when he hears his brothers express guilt over what they did to him years earlier?

The brothers are sent home with an abundance of grain. Despite the brothers' harm to him years earlier, Joseph responds to them with kindness and even returns the silver used as payment.

When have you experienced extraordinary kindness from someone else?

When have you offered unexpected kindness to someone else?

The brothers' guilty consciences make Joseph's kindness appear sinister to them.

Read Genesis 42:28. How do the brothers respond to the discovery of the silver?

The brothers return home and tell their father everything. All are afraid. But when they run out of grain, they run out of options. A return to Egypt is essential for survival. That's when Judah steps up and takes personal responsibility for Benjamin. Jacob sends his sons back to Egypt with the best items from their land and twice the silver they'd taken before. When Joseph sees his brothers, he orders a lavish feast. Once again, the brothers mistake Joseph's kind act as a sinister one, fearing they'll be imprisoned over the "stolen" silver.

Read Genesis 43:18–23. What is Joseph's response to the brothers' concern regarding the silver?

Then Joseph brings Simeon out. The brothers bow two more times to Joseph just as he had dreamed (verses 26, 28).

Read Genesis 43:29–31. How does Joseph respond to seeing Benjamin?

After the meal, the brothers are sent home with an abundance of food and the double portion of the silver they'd brought. But Joseph also tucked one of his own silver goblets into Benjamin's bag. Once his brothers depart, Joseph sends his steward after them to confront them about stealing the silver cup. In this, Joseph is testing his brothers to see if they've truly changed.

The brothers soon stand before Joseph again begging for mercy. Joseph tells them they can all leave—as long Benjamin stays. They face the same choice of abandoning their brother (as they had with Joseph decades before).

Read Genesis 44:30–31, 33–34. What does Judah offer to do to resolve the situation?

What does this reveal about the transformation that has happened in Judah's life?

> Judah advocated for his father and for his innocent young brother. He did what he should have done in the first place.

The siblings Joseph knew as a boy have been transformed. That's when Joseph drops the biggest reveal of all time.

Read Genesis 45:3–8. What does Joseph declare about the goodness of God in this passage?

How does Joseph's response to his brothers demonstrate grace and forgiveness rather than anger and revenge?

Read Romans 8:28. How is this principle demonstrated in Joseph's life?

Joseph instructs his brothers to go home and return to Egypt with the whole family, promising them the rich land of Goshen in which to settle (Genesis 45:10).

Read Genesis 45:14–15 and 46:29–30. Which of the following emotions likely surged through Joseph and his family members at their reunion? Circle all that apply.

Relief	Joy	Guardedness	Love	Exhaustion
Tenderness	Nostalgia	Gratitude	Surprise	Awkwardness

What does the reuniting of Joseph with his family reveal about the possibility of reconciliation when God is involved?

Joseph's journey is marked by great highs and lows. Yet through this journey, he helps provide salvation for his family and people everywhere. Throughout Joseph's story, we see him becoming the patriarch his brothers couldn't be. And through his service to the king and the kindness he shows his brothers, Joseph becomes a more righteous father than he himself had known. Indeed, God uses what was intended for evil to bring about great good.

On the continuum below, mark how many trusted relationships or institutions have let you down.

I've had few to no trusted relationships or institutions fail me. ○—○—○—○—○—○—○ I've had many trusted relationships or institutions fail me.

In the space below, write a prayer asking God to heal any areas where others' failures have impacted your ability to love, trust, and serve others.

Connect

Now that you've read and reflected on much of Joseph's story, it's time to connect this person of the Bible with your own life. Fill out the chart below.

What does Joseph's story teach you about overcoming family trauma?	
What challenges or encourages you most in Joseph's story?	
What does Joseph's story reveal about God working for your good when you can't see it?	
How do you hope to walk in greater trust in God and His goodness after studying the life of Joseph?	

Reveal

Now that you've connected Joseph's story with your own life, it's time to look at how God reveals His character and faithfulness to Joseph and how God is doing the same for you.

Where do you see God show up in Joseph's story, and what does that reveal about God?	
What does God reveal to you about His character and faithfulness through the life of Joseph?	
What does Joseph's story suggest or reveal about the way God wants to heal you and your relationships?	

Pray

Take a few minutes to ask the Holy Spirit to guide you as you respond to the following prayer prompts.

Lord, like Joseph, help me . . .

Lord, who are You prompting me to pursue reconciliation with? What's the next step I need to take in pursuing reconciliation, even if it's just praying and waiting?

Lord, where have You been at work bringing about good in my life that I haven't recognized yet?

Lord, considering Joseph's story, how are You calling me to live differently?

LESSON FIVE

Jonah's Anger

God gave [Jonah] a clear directive, but instead of obeying, Jonah turned and ran in the opposite direction—away from what God had called him to do. How dare he!? But the truth is, there's plenty in Jonah's story that applies to me—and may apply to you, too. . . . Like many other key stories in Scripture, Jonah's isn't a perfect fairy tale. It's full of disobedience, whining, and ultimately—redemption.

SHANNON BREAM

from *Nothing Is Impossible with God*

One of the great gifts of the Bible is that we encounter people who struggle with the same emotions as we do. While the details of our lives differ, we've all felt a surge of anger, a wave of fury. Jonah felt these emotions and more in frustration over what God had called him to do. He wanted to be anywhere else than where God wanted him, so he did what we sometimes do and ran in the opposite direction.

Yet Jonah's stubbornness was no match for God. Neither fear for his life nor prejudice toward a particular people could stand in the way of God's purposes. This is good news for us! Even when we remain faith*less*, God remains faith*full* and will accomplish His redemptive work in our lives and the world.

Reflect

The word of the Lord comes to Jonah in a direct, succinct way. Jonah receives the instruction to go to the big city of Nineveh and preach against it because of its great wickedness (Jonah 1:1–2).

Now, here's what's fascinating: Jonah never says a word. He doesn't protest or petition God for a different assignment. Nor does he argue for an alternative outcome. One might think he doesn't hear God at all, except for his strong reaction. He turns and bolts in the opposite direction.

Read Jonah 1:3–4. What actions did Jonah take to avoid obeying God?

Have you ever "paid your own way," so to speak, to avoid what God was calling you to do? If so, write about it.

Most scholars believe Tarshish was in modern-day Spain, making the journey roughly twenty-five hundred miles. Jonah puts distance between himself and God's mission and figures out an elaborate way to procrastinate.

In what areas are you prone to procrastination?

Where are you most prone to practice spiritual procrastination?

It's easy to pick on Jonah for refusing God's assignment, but history tells us he had a great reason. The Ninevites were part of the Assyrian Empire and were well-known for their horrific brutality. They were famed for gouging out eyes, cutting off limbs, and skinning people alive. No wonder Jonah wants nothing to do with them, let alone becoming an itinerant preacher there.

Once aboard the ship, Jonah soon wakes up to trouble. A storm hits, and amid the raging water, the pagan captain and crew members call on every god they can think of to save them. When none of them do, they wake up Jonah and ask him to call on his God.

Read Jonah 1:4–6 and Matthew 8:24–26. What parallels do you see between Jonah's response to the storm and Jesus' response to the storm?

> While Jonah would need to sacrifice himself to quiet the sea,
> Jesus did not—He is master of the waves Himself.

Read Jonah 1:7–10. How does Jonah identify himself, and how does the crew respond?

Despite Jonah's disobedience, God's presence and mercy are evident in Jonah's life and the lives of those he is with.

Read Jonah 1:11–17. What does Jonah tell the crew they must do to calm the storm?

It's an impossible situation, but once again, God makes the impossible possible. A large fish swallows the prophet, and he sits in its belly for three days and nights. The time frame and imagery foreshadow Jesus' once-and-for-all rescue to come.

Read Matthew 12:40–41. What does Jesus say about Jonah and His own death and resurrection?

Sometimes God's provision doesn't instantly fix everything or make life more comfortable. It may not look like anything we'd choose or want. Yet just as God worked through Jonah in that time and place, He can work through our situations too. Jonah offers a surprising and beautiful prayer from the belly of that fish.

Read Jonah 2:1–9. What does Jonah declare about God in his prayer?

What do Jonah's declarations reveal about the transformation taking place within him?

What "fish" has the Lord allowed you to sit in as a result of your spiritual procrastination or disobedience?

What observation does the prophet make in verse 8? How has this been true in your life?

The great fish vomits Jonah onto the shore—stinky seaweed and all. God instructs Jonah once again to go to Nineveh. This time, he obeys.

Read Jonah 3:1–10. How do the Ninevites respond to Jonah's eight-word message?

How does the Ninevites' quick response to God compare to Jonah's initial response to God?

Moved by the repentance of the Ninevites, God has mercy on them. The response would bring overwhelming joy to most preachers. But Jonah gets upset.

Read Jonah 4:1–5. Why is Jonah so mad and depressed?

How does God respond to Jonah's complaint?

God demonstrates His loving compassion time and time again—to the sailors, to the people of Nineveh, and to Jonah. Yet the prophet's heart remains hard. It's easy to point fingers at Jonah, but we must look at our own hearts. Sometimes we, too, have bad attitudes and feel that our joy has been stolen when the wicked prosper. But that doesn't give us license to assume they are wholly evil and beyond God's merciful redemption.

Who or what are you struggling with today because it appears that the wicked are prospering?

Read Jonah 4:6–11. How does God use a plant to communicate, teach, and illustrate a greater truth to Jonah?

Where are you allowing your anger and prejudice to blind you to the redemptive work of God?

Jesus gave His life for the very worst among us and the very worst in us. The apostle Paul reminds us that the mercy of God knows no bounds.

Read Colossians 3:11–14. What barriers are eliminated by Jesus' death, resurrection, and salvation?

How are we supposed to live in light of what Jesus has done for us?

Through the highly resistant prophet Jonah, God throws the Ninevites a lifeline. In Jonah's day, they humble themselves and turn toward Him. In later generations, they return to evil and it becomes their ultimate downfall. The invitation to redemption will continue through all generations until God makes all things new. Until then, He'll keep calling for Jonahs to go to the Ninevehs of the world. Let's plan on saying yes—and walking in obedience rather than anger, mercy instead of being mad.

On the continuum below, indicate how much you struggle with anger toward those who perpetrate injustice or cruelty in this world.

I find I frequently struggle with those who perpetrate injustice or cruelty in this world. — ○ — ○ — ○ — ○ — ○ — ○ — ○ — I find I'm hopeful and prayerful toward those who perpetrate injustice or cruelty in this world.

In the space below, write any names or situations where you struggle to believe God can bring repentance and restoration. Then ask God to help you be a beacon of prayer and hope to them.

Connect

Now that you've read and reflected on much of Jonah's story, it's time to connect this person of the Bible with your own life. Fill out the chart below.

What does Jonah's story teach you about the mercy you've received from God?	
What challenges or encourages you most in Jonah's story?	
What does Jonah's story reveal to you about overcoming impossible situations?	
How do you hope to walk in greater trust in God after studying the life of Jonah?	

Reveal

Now that you've connected Jonah's story with your own life, it's time to look at how God reveals His character and faithfulness to Jonah and how God is doing the same for you.

Where do you see God show up in Jonah's life, and what does that reveal about God?	
What does God reveal to you about His character and faithfulness through the life of Jonah?	
What does Jonah's story suggest or reveal to you about the way God wants to use you?	

Pray

Take a few minutes to ask the Holy Spirit to guide you as you respond to the following prayer prompts.

Lord, like Jonah, help me . . .

Lord, where have I judged others as beyond Your mercy or redemption? How am I resisting loving those to whom You are calling me?

Lord, where am I secretly (or blatantly) angry with You and what You've done (or left undone)? How do You want to transform me and my perspective?

Lord, considering Jonah's story, how are You calling me to live with greater obedience to You and mercy toward others?

LESSON SIX

Daniel's Integrity

The Lord knew Daniel and his friends would be stripped away from their families and the lives they knew and taken to Babylon. It wasn't a turn of events meant to punish them. Instead, . . . it set up numerous opportunities for the Lord to be glorified far beyond the borders of where the Jewish people were living at the time.

SHANNON BREAM
from *Nothing Is Impossible with God*

Daniel and his three friends were carried away from Jerusalem to Babylon. Scholars suggest that every effort was made to indoctrinate them into the Babylonian lifestyle. Yet they remained steadfast. Their story teaches us that integrity is worth fighting for, even in the most difficult situations.

Reflect

Following the Babylonians' invasion of Jerusalem, King Nebuchadnezzar orders that male Israelites from the royal family and high nobility be brought back to serve in his palace. Daniel and his three friends—Hananiah, Mishael, and Azariah—are among those forced into lifelong service to the king and kingdom.

Almost every detail of their lives is orchestrated for them, including their amount of daily food and wine from the king's table. Yet the food isn't kosher—literally or figuratively—and had likely been offered to idols. Daniel requests that he and his friends be allowed to abstain from the menu. But Ashpenaz, the chief official entrusted with Daniel's care, worries that he'll be the one to pay the price if they don't look as healthy or strong as the other young men in training.

Read Daniel 1:11–16. What deal did Daniel negotiate with the guard assigned to him?

How is Daniel's humble refusal to compromise rewarded?

God's protection, provision, and favor for Daniel and his friends extends well beyond the physical.

Read Daniel 1:17–20. In what other ways does God provide for Daniel and his friends?

After Daniel and his friends are placed into royal service, the king has a disturbing dream and demands an interpretation. Yet he refuses to tell anyone the details of the dream.

The king is infuriated when his astrologers tell him it's impossible. He pledges to destroy all the wise men in his service. When the king's guard comes to execute Daniel, he asks the king for more time.

Read Daniel 2:17–23. What role do prayer and friendship play in the dream's interpretation?

What attributes of God does Daniel highlight in his praise-filled response?

Daniel rushes back to the king's guard with the king's dream and its interpretation. Yet he doesn't just plead for his life and the lives of his friends; he calls on the king to preserve the lives of the wise men of Babylon (verse 24).

Read Daniel 2:27–28. What does Daniel want the most powerful man in the land to know about the source of his dream?

Daniel proceeds to outline every detail of the dream and its meaning.

Read Daniel 2:46–49. How does the king respond to Daniel's dream interpretation?

How does Daniel advocate for his friends?

Despite the king's favor, Daniel's three friends, who have been renamed Shadrach, Meshach, and Abednego, find themselves in another impossible situation.

King Nebuchadnezzar, who loves gold and loves himself, has a giant gold statue constructed. He demands that everyone, everywhere bow down and worship the statue whenever specific music is played. Those who refuse will be tossed into a blazing furnace. Some astrologists inform the king that Shadrach, Meshach, and Abednego have refused his orders. The king is enraged.

Read Daniel 3:13–18. How do the three Jewish men respond to King Nebuchadnezzar?

What characteristics do they display in the face of an impossible situation?

Which of these characteristics would you most like to have? Why?

The king orders the furnace heated seven times hotter than normal—so hot that those who throw Shadrach, Meshach, and Abednego into the blistering flames die instantly (Daniel 3:22). When Nebuchadnezzar looks in, he's shocked to see four "men" walking in the fire. Whether the fourth figure in the fire is an angel or an incarnation of God Himself we do not know, but we can clearly see miraculous protection.

When the furnace doors open, the Bible notes that the men's hair isn't singed nor do their clothes carry the slightest whiff of smoke. Once again, Nebuchadnezzar finds himself astonished at the work of God among his Jewish captives.

Read Daniel 3:28–30. What does Nebuchadnezzar discover about God through this encounter?

The friendship of Shadrach, Meshach, and Abednego teaches us the powerful role community can play in maintaining integrity. Those around us can help us stand strong when we feel the weakest.

What role does community play in maintaining your integrity?

Who encourages you to stay faithful and true to all that God has commanded?

How can you build more friendships like that one?

Several years later, Nebuchadnezzar has another disturbing dream. Once again, no one can interpret it except for Daniel. But the dream's prophetic message is the last thing the king wants to hear.

The dream sequence compares the king to a mighty tree that will be chopped down with only a stump and its roots remaining. The king will lose his sanity for seven years and wander like a wild animal until he finally acknowledges God as the one true ruler of all.

Read Daniel 4:27. What two things does Daniel urge the king to do in response to the dream?

King Nebuchadnezzar refuses Daniel's wisdom, and his dream becomes a living nightmare. The once-hailed king becomes an unrecognizable figure. Then, seven years later, just as predicted, the king's sanity returns.

Read Daniel 4:34–37. What does King Nebuchadnezzar proclaim about God after his restoration?

How is King Nebuchadnezzar transformed through this experience?

> The most unlikely person in the world, the *least* exiled person, identified with God's exiles after experiencing an exile of his own.

You might think this was the end of Daniel's story, but God establishes Daniel in Babylon for leaders still to come. Eventually, Belshazzar becomes king. Nebuchadnezzar's successor foolishly orders that the golden goblets from the temple in Jerusalem be used at his party. When he and his guests drink from the sacred vessels, a terrifying image shocks them into silence.

The fingers of a human hand appear and write on the wall. The king's face turns white as a sheet. Petrified, he calls on the astrologers and wise men of Babylon and promises great wealth to whoever can interpret the imagery. No one can.

Read Daniel 5:13–17. How does the king describe Daniel? What reward does he offer Daniel?

What does Daniel's response to the king's offer reveal about his integrity?

Daniel reminds Belshazzar of how his predecessor, King Nebuchadnezzar, became arrogant with power. Then Daniel interprets the handwriting and predicts Belshazzar's fate.

Read Daniel 5:22–30. What has Belshazzar done wrong? What is the outcome of his attitudes and actions?

As Daniel predicts, Belshazzar's reign ends and the kingdom is divided. The rulers of Babylon continue to change, but Daniel's favor in the kingdom remains.

When we see Daniel in the sixth chapter, his youthful years have long vanished. He's now in his eighties. He's seen kings come and go. Empires grow stronger and then crumble. Yet he's never lost his faith and devotion to God.

When Darius the Mede takes over the empire, he promotes Daniel. This riles up the governors and administrators. They puff up the king with flattery and then unveil a duplicitous plan. They convince King Darius to issue a decree that anyone who prays to anyone except the king will be thrown into the lions' den, knowing full well that Daniel will never bend his knee.

Read Daniel 6:10–13. How does Daniel respond to the edict, and what is the outcome?

Read Daniel 6:14. What does the king's response reveal about how he views Daniel?

Darius's hands are tied, and he orders the elderly Daniel to be thrown to the lions. The king petitions, "May your God, whom you serve continually, rescue you!" (Daniel 6:16). At dawn, he races to the lions' den.

Read Daniel 6:20–23. How did God protect Daniel?

What is the king's response?

Daniel never returns his enemy's hatred with hatred. He simply keeps returning to God with prayer, humility, and faithfulness. Daniel's life is marked by honor and integrity and strengthened by deep relationships with fellow believers. Daniel reminds us to serve God no matter the outcome.

Take a moment and think about the trickiest situation you're facing at work, at home, or in your finances. On the continuum below, mark how much you struggle with maintaining your integrity in that circumstance.

I find it easy to maintain my integrity and do what is right. ○—○—○—○—○—○—○ I find it's hard to maintain my integrity and do what is right.

In the space below, write a prayer asking God to give you the strength and strategy to maintain your integrity and do what is right in this situation.

Connect

Now that you've read and reflected on much of Daniel's story, it's time to connect this person of the Bible with your own life. Fill out the chart below.

What does Daniel's story teach you about integrity and faithfulness to God?	
What challenges or encourages you most in Daniel's story?	
What does Daniel's story reveal to you about overcoming impossible situations?	
How do you hope to walk in greater confidence in God after studying the life of Daniel?	

Reveal

Now that you've connected Daniel's story with your own life, it's time to look at how God reveals His character and faithfulness to Daniel and how God is doing the same for you.

Where do you see God show up in Daniel's life, and what does that reveal about God?	
What does God reveal to you about His character and faithfulness through the life of Daniel?	
What does Daniel's story suggest or reveal about the way you can best honor God right now?	

Pray

Take a few minutes to ask the Holy Spirit to guide you as you respond to the following prayer prompts.

Lord, like Daniel, help me . . .

Lord, where am I allowing little compromises and concessions into my life that are drawing me away from You? What changes do I need to make to live in full allegiance to You?

Lord, where am I turning other than You for the answers in my life? What do I need to entrust to You through prayer right now?

Lord, considering Daniel's story, how are You calling me to live differently?

LESSON SEVEN

Nehemiah's Wisdom

[Nehemiah] didn't seek out the spotlight, and he didn't even take credit for his plan . . .; instead, he said it was all God's idea. . . . He wasn't distracted by petty accusations or sidetracked into quarreling with his enemies on their own terms.

SHANNON BREAM
from *Nothing Is Impossible with God*

Have you ever had a dream of doing something that seemed impossible? Maybe it was a financial goal or traveling to a particular place. Maybe for you it involved making a difference, finishing a race, or completing a project.

Nehemiah had a dream to rebuild a wall in a city he'd never even visited before. The mission would require finding great favor, navigating difficult people, overcoming internal doubts, and addressing external sabotage. Yet through God's wisdom, Nehemiah watches the impossible become possible and witnesses a spiritual revival he never could have imagined.

Reflect

When we meet Nehemiah, he's the cupbearer to the king. In antiquity, cupbearers were high-ranking, trusted individuals responsible for drinking (and sometimes eating) portions of each royal meal to ensure its safety. With the constant threat of assassinations through poisoning, cupbearers held the life of the king in their hands. Due to their proximity to royalty, they often became confidants and advisors, influencing the king's political decisions.

Read Nehemiah 1:1–4. What is Nehemiah's reaction to the news regarding Jerusalem?

What does this reveal about Nehemiah's faith?

Nehemiah was born in captivity. Though he has never set foot in Jerusalem, he grieves when he hears about the condition of the city where his fellow Jews are trying to rebuild their lives.

Read Nehemiah 1:5–11. Reflect on his prayer and fill in the chart below.

How does Nehemiah describe God?	
What does Nehemiah confess?	
What part of God's promise does Nehemiah point out in verses 8–9?	
What does Nehemiah ask for?	

What roles do praise, confession, remembering God's promises, and petitions play in your prayer life?

No matter a person's role in the palace, it was unfavorable, if not downright illegal, to enter the king's presence in anything other than a cheerful mood. So King Artaxerxes is taken aback by Nehemiah's sad countenance.

Read Nehemiah 2:1–8. What does Nehemiah ask of the king, and how does King Artaxerxes respond?

Nehemiah heads to Jerusalem with the king's blessing and protection, but opposition soon arises.

Read Nehemiah 2:10. Why do Sanballat and Tobiah oppose Nehemiah?

Rather than dive straight into the massive construction project, Nehemiah walks in wisdom by taking time to evaluate all that needs to be done. Only after this thorough review does Nehemiah gather the people.

Read Nehemiah 2:17–18. What reasons does Nehemiah give for rebuilding the wall? How do the people respond?

It doesn't take long for Nehemiah's enemies to rise up, mock him, and undermine his reason for being in Jerusalem.

Read Nehemiah 2:19–20. What wisdom does Nehemiah show in his response?

Are there any areas of your life where drama or pointless arguments are stealing your time and attention?

How can you walk in greater wisdom and restraint like Nehemiah?

As the building project continues, Nehemiah's opponents become more vocal, their insults dripping with discouragement and defeat.

Read Nehemiah 4:1–6. What wisdom does Nehemiah show in how he responds to threats from Sanballat and Tobiah?

What begins as mockery and taunting soon transitions into threats of physical violence. Unease spreads throughout the land, and the temptation to preemptively start a battle looms large.

Read Nehemiah 4:7–23. What concerns do the people express, and how does Nehemiah address each one?

The opposition that begins externally soon surfaces internally. Some members of the Jewish community take advantage of their brothers and sisters who, while trying to rebuild their lives, are being obligated to pay taxes to the Persian Empire.

Read Nehemiah 5:1–6. What are the people's outcries and complaints?

Read Nehemiah 5:7–13. How does Nehemiah respond?

How does this bring healing to the community?

The leadership Nehemiah provides entitles him to lavish perks including food, wine, and luxuries—all funded by taxes. Even though Nehemiah has the legal right to enjoy these privileges, he refuses.

Read Nehemiah 5:14–19. What wisdom does Nehemiah display regarding the trappings of his role?

What does this reveal about the work of God in Nehemiah's life?

What's one thing you're saying no to because even though it's legal or allowed, it could become a snare to others or distract you from what God has called you to do?

Meanwhile, Sanballat and Tobiah continue scheming. At one point they go on a smear campaign and make up a story about Nehemiah doing all of this just so he can become king. Another time, they hire someone to deliver a false prophecy and intimidate him with a death threat. Nehemiah has every human reason to fret and fear, yet he keeps returning to God in prayer, trusting Him with the outcome.

In the face of increasing opposition, the wall is completed in fifty-two days (Nehemiah 6:15). Through Nehemiah and his Jewish community, God accomplished the impossible.

Read Nehemiah 6:16. How do the surrounding nations respond to the completion of the wall?

The wall was just part of what needed to be rebuilt in Jerusalem. The spiritual condition and morale of the people also needed an overhaul. Everyone listens intently when the prophet Ezra reads the book of the law of Moses from daybreak until noon.

Read Nehemiah 8:5–12. What does the people's emotional response reveal about their spiritual state?

The people's jubilant spiritual renewal is marked by deep repentance as they recognize their sins and turn from them (Nehemiah 9:2). Though they have broken covenant with God, they recognize His faithfulness and renew their commitment to study His Word and obey His commandments.

Read Nehemiah 10:30–39. What promises do the people make? How do these promises ensure they don't neglect their relationships with God?

With the physical walls and the spiritual framework in place, families begin repopulating Jerusalem. Nehemiah returns to his service to King Artaxerxes. All seems well, until Nehemiah hears of trouble brewing in Jerusalem. And you'll never guess the culprits!

Tobiah and Sanballat sneakily compromise the high priest Eliashib. Sanballat's daughter marries Eliashib's grandson (Nehemiah 13:28). And Tobiah has been given "a room in the courts of the house of God" (Nehemiah 13:7)—a serious breach of sacred space.

Read Nehemiah 13:8–9. What does Nehemiah do upon his return to Jerusalem?

> Nehemiah could have stayed at the king's palace in Persia. He could have plausibly argued that he'd already done the work God called him to. . . . But he didn't.

When Nehemiah discovers the people violating God's law by breaking the Sabbath, he shuts the city gates and ends trade temporarily. He demands immediate reform by those who have married outside their religious community.

Time and time again, Nehemiah demonstrates wisdom through decisive action and separating the people from corrupting influences. He prioritizes spiritual purity over personal popularity.

Nehemiah understood that the goal of restoration was not just rebuilding a city, but rebuilding a relationship with God, which means living a distinct lifestyle. While Nehemiah's repeated attempts to restore the Jewish people's spiritual connection with God weren't perfect, the One who would come centuries later would finally restore the people's hearts to God once and for all—as He will for all who come to Him.

On the continuum below, mark how easy or hard it is for you to dream big in the face of opposition.

I find it easy to dream big in the face of opposition. ○—○—○—○—○—○—○ I find it hard to dream big in the face of opposition.

In the space below, write a prayer asking God to focus your vision on what He wants to accomplish in your life. Ask Him to strengthen your faith when opposition or discouragement arise.

Connect

Now that you've read and reflected on much of Nehemiah's story, it's time to connect this person of the Bible with your own life. Fill out the chart below.

What does Nehemiah's story teach you about your ongoing need for God's wisdom?	
What challenges or encourages you most in Nehemiah's story?	
What does Nehemiah's story reveal to you about navigating opposition and discouragement?	
How do you hope to walk in greater wisdom with God after studying the life of Nehemiah?	

Reveal

Now that you've connected Nehemiah's story with your own life, it's time to look at how God reveals His character and faithfulness to Nehemiah and how God is doing the same for you.

Where do you see God show up in Nehemiah's life, and what does that reveal about God?	
What does God reveal to you about His character and faithfulness through the life of Nehemiah?	
What does Nehemiah's story suggest or reveal about the way God wants to use you?	

Pray

Take a few minutes to ask the Holy Spirit to guide you as you respond to the following prayer prompts.

Lord, like Nehemiah, help me . . .

Lord, what are You calling me to do that seems impossible in this season? What's the next right step I need to take?

Lord, where am I most tempted to do things on my own rather than listen and yield to Your wisdom?

Lord, considering Nehemiah's story, how are You calling me to live differently?

LESSON EIGHT

Noah's Patience

Because of Noah's faith, you and
I are here. . . . He wasn't perfect . . .
but that didn't keep the Lord from
using Noah—an encouragement
for every one of us flawed
children of God.

SHANNON BREAM
from *Nothing Is Impossible with God*

The Lord chooses Noah to rescue humanity. But God's plan doesn't unfold on Noah's timeline or in any way he could have anticipated. Noah's story reminds us that following God requires patience, and waiting on God will always bring about the best outcome.

Reflect

From the beginning, every human is fearfully and wonderfully made in the image of God. Our Creator intends that we will walk with Him, enjoy and care for His creation, and reflect His glory. But by the time we meet Noah, humanity has become defined by violence, corruption, and evil.

Read Genesis 6:5–8. What does this passage reveal about the depths of humanity's depravation?

What does verse 8 reveal about Noah?

At this point, humanity faces two threats: overwhelming evil and an impending flood. Through Noah, God maps out a way to overcome both. But what Noah is asked to build makes no sense by human standards.

Read Genesis 6:14–16. What are the specifications for Noah's construction project?

When have you sensed the Lord asking you to do something that didn't make sense from a human perspective? What was the outcome?

> Stories of God's judgment should not lead us to despair. Don't ever let anyone—including yourself—tell you that you're too far gone, that your story is too messy to be redeemed.

Read Genesis 6:17–22. What does the Lord inform Noah will happen?

What are the Lord's unique instructions for survival, and how does Noah respond?

Read Hebrews 11:1, 7. What enabled Noah to take a risk and follow God when no one else did?

Finally, the time Noah has been faithfully working toward arrives.

Read Genesis 7:1–12. What does it reveal about God's character that He gives Noah and his family seven days of advance notice of the flood that's coming?

Read Genesis 7:17–24. What is required of Noah and his family during the 150 days the water flooded the earth?

What challenges do you suspect they faced during that time? Circle any that apply.

Boredom	Noise	Fear	Exhaustion
Extreme odor	Confinement	Seasickness	Other:____________

How difficult is it for you to remain patient during times of waiting?

Eventually, the ark rests on the "mountains of Ararat" (Genesis 8:4) as the water recedes and the mountaintops appear. What follows echoes the creation sequence, as God again separates the earth from the water in set periods of time. Little by little, God shows Noah the life to come. The first time Noah sends out a bird, it returns to the ark because there's nowhere for it to land.

Read Genesis 8:10–12. How does the dove respond each time Noah sends it out? What does each return reveal about the condition of the land?

By most calculations, Noah and his family spend roughly one year on the ark. We know this now, but for Noah and his family it probably felt like forever. They didn't know if they'd be aboard a few months or many years—and when you're in it, the long tunnel of waiting can seem like it will never end.

Read Genesis 8:15–22. What does the Lord instruct Noah to do, and how does Noah respond?

What does it show about Noah and his relationship with God that his first act is to build an altar and worship the Lord?

What is your first act or response following a long season of waiting on God?

How does God respond to Noah's sacrificial act?

Genesis 9 begins with the Lord giving Noah and his descendants dominion over everything on the earth. He also warns that human life is precious. After this warning, our Creator outlines His covenant with the one righteous family He chose to save, a promise that resembles the later covenants to Abraham, Israel, and the church, affirming God's unchanging character.

Read Genesis 9:9–17. What promises does God make?

The ark is a picture of the salvation that comes through Jesus. Just as it was in the days of Noah, our world is marred by evil. Everywhere we look, there are distortions of the peace and splendor God has planned for us. Corruption abounds, but there is also a permanent way of escape. Jesus is our vessel of deliverance!

Read Genesis 9:20–27. What mistake does Noah make, and how does this leave him vulnerable?

What does Noah do when he wakes up and discovers what has happened?

What Noah declares plays out in generations to come. Yet despite his moment of weakness, Noah is remembered as "a preacher of righteousness" (2 Peter 2:5). Noah teaches us that we can patiently wait on God in the toughest circumstances, even if it makes us look foolish for a time.

On the continuum below, mark how much you struggle with remaining patient when you're waiting on God.

I find it easy to remain patient. ○—○—○—○—○—○—○ I find it hard to remain patient.

In the space below, write a prayer asking God to give you more patience as you wait on Him.

Connect

Now that you've read and reflected on much of Noah's story, it's time to connect this person from the Bible with your own life. Fill out the chart below.

What does Noah's story teach you about the importance of patience?	
What challenges or encourages you most in Noah's story?	
What does Noah's story reveal to you about God making a way where there appears to be no way?	
How do you hope to walk in greater faith in God after studying the life of Noah?	

Reveal

Now that you've connected Noah's story with your own life, it's time to look at how God reveals His character and faithfulness to Noah and how God is doing the same for you.

Where do you see God show up in Noah's life, and what does that reveal about God?	
What does God reveal to you about His character and faithfulness through the life of Noah?	
What does Noah's story suggest or reveal about the way God wants to use you?	

Pray

Take a few minutes to ask the Holy Spirit to guide you as you respond to the following prayer prompts.

Lord, like Noah, help me . . .

Lord, where in my life am I "aboard the ark," waiting for You to do what only You can do? How can I grow in patience?

Lord, where am I most tempted to take matters into my own hands or jump ahead of Your timetable? How can I learn to wait well?

Lord, considering Noah's story, how are You calling me to live differently?

LESSON NINE

Joshua's Obedience

Joshua had already shown himself to be strong and courageous, but even God's most devoted children need assurance from time to time. . . . Moses repeatedly petitioned the Lord on behalf of the people, and he had finally led them to the cusp of where they'd always been meant to be. But it would be Joshua who would take them across the finish line.

SHANNON BREAM

from *Nothing Is Impossible with God*

The Bible reveals that we are part of a greater story that God is writing throughout history and the world. While Moses helped free the Israelites from slavery in Egypt and led them through the desert, ultimately, he would not be the one to lead them into the promised land. That role would be fulfilled by one of the leaders Moses helped raise up: Joshua.

Yet crossing the finish line into appointed land wasn't without significant challenges. Joshua, alongside Caleb, discovered what many long-distance runners know: Sometimes the last steps are the hardest ones. Yet through radical obedience, Joshua and Caleb helped God's people settle in the promised place.

Reflect

On their way out of Egypt and through the wilderness, the Israelites witness miracle after miracle. They watch the ten plagues, experience the protection of their firstborns, and pass through the Red Sea. They're guided by a pillar of cloud by day and fire by night, drink bitter water that is made sweet, survive on manna, and watch the defeat of the Amalekites as long as Moses's hands are raised.

During their four decades in the desert, neither their clothing nor sandals wear out. They experience the power and presence of God—His protection, provision, and guidance. Yet, like many of us, the people of Israel are quick to forget what God has done when they face yet another challenge.

On the edge of the promised land, the Lord instructs Moses to send some men into Canaan to scout the land and its resources. When the twelve spies return, they report oversized fruit, great abundance, and that the territory has everything they'll need to thrive. Then ten of the spies drop a discouragement bombshell.

Read Numbers 13:28–33. What obstacles to entering the promised land do the ten spies list?

Two of the spies, Joshua and Caleb, believe that God will come through for His people. Despite their courageous rebuttal, fearful rumors spread throughout the camp. The community has a meltdown.

Read Numbers 14:1–4. How do the Israelites respond to the ten spies' report?

Read Numbers 14:6–9. How do Joshua and Caleb respond to the people?

Joshua and Caleb hold firm to their faith in God and readiness to obey Him. Yet the people of Israel want to stone them. When the Lord, angered by the people's response, shows up, Moses intercedes for the people.

Because of the Israelites' unwillingness to move forward, the Lord decides to send them backward. He tells Moses to head back toward the wilderness (verse 25) with a difficult message: No one aged twenty years or older (except for Joshua and Caleb) will enter the promised land (verse 29). The people's grumbling wish to die in the wilderness is granted. Then God strikes down the ten spies who delivered the negative, fear-filled report that sparked the people's defiance.

Read Numbers 14:40–45. How do the Israelites continue to defy God's instructions? What is the result?

As the Israelites trudge through the wilderness, the Lord instructs Moses to designate Joshua as his successor (Numbers 27:18–23). He gives specific instructions regarding their arrival in Canaan.

Read Numbers 33:50–56. What does the Lord command the people to do?

After forty years in the wilderness, Joshua becomes the leader of the Israelites. As the book of Joshua opens, the Lord speaks to Joshua regarding his future.

Read Joshua 1:3–9. What promises does the Lord make to Joshua?

How do these instructions and promises reveal God's loving presence?

Which of the promises made to Joshua do you most need to hear in your current situation?

God tucks the keys to success into His directions to Joshua: *Don't get distracted. Stay on target. Meditate on My truth day and night.* It's really a simple formula, if we'll just commit ourselves to it—and Joshua did. Next, Joshua tells the people to prepare to cross the Jordan River.

Read Joshua 1:14–18. What is the people's response to Joshua?

How have the people changed from the last time they stood on the border of the promised land?

> Taking the promised land wasn't about feeling confident that they could do so. It was about respecting and loving the God who had pledged to give it to them.

Before they enter the promised land, Joshua sends out another scouting mission. Instead of twelve spies, he sends two. They find refuge in the house of a prostitute named Rahab. She directs those hunting the spies on a wild-goose chase. In exchange, she asks the spies to protect her and her family when they invade.

Read Joshua 2:23–24. What report do the spies deliver?

How does this spies' report confirm what Caleb and Joshua had declared years earlier in Numbers 14:6–9?

The people are instructed to follow the ark of the covenant at a distance and consecrate themselves for the battle ahead.

Read Joshua 3:5. What promise does Joshua give the people regarding God?

Joshua obeys the Lord's guidance to a T, directing the priests to carry the ark of the covenant and step into the Jordan River. As soon as the priests dip their toes in the water, something miraculous and reminiscent of the miracle at the Red Sea happens.

Read Joshua 3:15–17 and 4:15–18. How do the waters respond to the priests entering and exiting the river?

The people of Israel gather twelve stones from the middle of the Jordan, where the priests are standing with the ark (Joshua 4:8).

Read Joshua 4:19–24. What is the significance of these stones of remembrance?

Take a moment to reflect on three times when you've sensed, seen, or encountered God's provision, protection, or guidance in your life. Make a few notes about each in the space below.

1

2

3

Why is it important or meaningful to remember these markers of God's faithfulness to you?

How does remembering what God did in the past strengthen your faith for what you're facing in the present?

As word of the miraculous event began to spread, so did fear of the Lord. The Amorite and Canaanite kings "lost heart and their courage failed because of the Israelites" (Joshua 5:1 CSB). Then the Lord instructs Joshua that all the men need to be circumcised as a sign of God's covenant with Abraham. Once again, Joshua obeys.

Soon the people of Israel face a battle for Jericho. God gives Joshua a battle plan containing highly unusual instructions.

Read Joshua 6:1–14. What instructions does God give Joshua, and how do the people respond?

Read Joshua 6:15–21. How does the people's obedience lead to victory?

Every living thing in the city of Jericho is destroyed, except for Rahab and those who took refuge in her home. This salvation story is so important that centuries later, we find Rahab listed in the genealogy of Christ in the opening of Matthew's gospel. But the inspiring story of Rahab's life may never have come to be had Joshua and Caleb not obeyed God in the face of overwhelming opposition.

Their obedience was quick because they knew God as Savior, Protector, Provider, and loving Father. It took repeated acts of courage, over many decades, before the victory Joshua and Caleb believed in actually happened. Yet they moved forward, buoyed by the command: "Be strong and courageous" (Joshua 10:25). And we can too.

On the continuum below, mark how much you struggle to remain strong and courageous where God has placed you.

I find it easy to remain strong and courageous every day. — ○ — ○ — ○ — ○ — ○ — ○ — ○ — I find it hard to remain strong and courageous every day.

In the space below, write a prayer asking God to remove any doubts and fears and replace them with confidence in Him.

Connect

Now that you've read and reflected on much of Joshua's story, it's time to connect this person of the Bible with your own life. Fill out the chart below.

What does Joshua's story teach you about holding on to optimism in a pessimist's world?	
What challenges or encourages you most in Joshua's story?	
What does Joshua's story reveal to you about the importance of obedience?	
How do you hope to walk in greater obedience to God after studying the life of Joshua?	

Reveal

Now that you've connected Joshua's story with your own life, it's time to look at how God reveals His character and faithfulness to Joshua and how God is doing the same for you.

Where do you see God show up in Joshua's life, and what does that reveal about God?	
What does God reveal to you about His character and faithfulness through the life of Joshua?	
What does Joshua's story suggest or reveal about the way God wants to use you?	

Pray

Take a few minutes to ask the Holy Spirit to guide you as you respond to the following prayer prompts.

Lord, like Joshua, help me . . .

Lord, where am I allowing discouragers and naysayers to shape my decisions and responses? How can I break free from any pessimistic perspectives that are eroding my faith in You?

Lord, where are You calling me to be stronger and more courageous?

Lord, considering Joshua's story, how are You calling me to live differently?

LESSON TEN

Elijah's Discouragement

[Elijah] is a man who followed God so faithfully and so closely that he never actually faced death. Instead, God sent a heavenly chariot to pick him up and take him to his eternal home (2 Kings 2:11). He was a conduit for incredible miracles and had the Lord's hand on his life. . . . Yet Elijah experienced deep discouragement and a feeling that he was the only one fighting for what was right and good. We know he was never truly alone, and neither are you.

SHANNON BREAM

from *Nothing Is Impossible with God*

God gives the prophet Elijah the challenging task of speaking out against the Baal worship that has spread throughout the land. His call to repent and return to the one true God draws fierce opposition and places him in the crosshairs of King Ahab and Queen Jezebel.

Despite the incredible miracles that mark his ministry—raising the dead, calling down fire from the sky, and parting the Jordan River, Elijah struggles with loneliness, discouragement, depression, and abandonment. His story reminds us that even in our darkest moments, the truth of God's Word and the reality of His presence can empower us to overcome.

Reflect

The prophet Elijah lives in a time when the nation of Israel is divided. The kingdom to the north is technically Israel, and to the south, the land is called Judah.

Read 1 Kings 16:30–33. How does King Ahab rebel against God?

Read 1 Kings 17:1. What message does Elijah deliver to King Ahab? What does it reveal about God?

After Elijah delivers the news to Ahab, God instructs Elijah to go to a place where he can hide from Ahab.

Read 1 Kings 17:2–6. How does God miraculously provide for Elijah in this isolated place?

Describe a time when God miraculously provided for you.

Sometimes God works the most deeply in our hearts when He has our undivided attention. Jesus reminds us of this truth following the death of John the Baptist.

Read Mark 6:30–32. Describe a time when you felt prompted to be alone so that God could do a work of healing or restoration in you.

Eventually, the brook that nourishes Elijah dries up, signaling it's time for the prophet to move on. The Lord instructs Elijah to go to Zarephath, the region Queen Jezebel is from and the heart of Baal-worshiping territory. God sends him to the most unlikely provider, a marginalized and impoverished widow.

Read 1 Kings 17:8–16. What's the first miracle God performs through Elijah for the widow?

Read 1 Kings 17:17–24. What's the second miracle God performs through Elijah for the widow?

What do these miracles reveal about the character of God?

Read Luke 4:25–26. What does Jesus say about the widow of Zarephath?

Following roughly three years of drought, the Lord instructs Elijah to return to King Ahab. Another brave man of God, Obadiah, brokers the meeting. But King Ahab isn't happy about seeing Elijah again.

Read 1 Kings 18:17–19. What does King Ahab call Elijah?

What does Elijah ask for in preparation for the showdown to come?

Ahab didn't like that Elijah was right about the three years of drought, and he certainly doesn't like the news Elijah delivers now. Yet he respects Elijah enough to follow his instructions and allow this showdown to take place on Mount Carmel.

Read 1 Kings 18:21–24. What is Elijah trying to accomplish through this showdown?

The prophets of Baal follow Elijah's directives, but the false god never shows up. It gets so bad that Elijah even resorts to some trash-talking.

Read 1 Kings 18:25–29. How does Elijah taunt the false prophets?

Before calling on the one true God, Elijah repairs the altar of the Lord. He gathers twelve stones, one for each tribe, and encourages the people to remember their identity.

Read 1 Kings 18:33–35. How does Elijah make God's task, setting the altar on fire, seem even more impossible?

Elijah's preparations and powerful prayers give all the credit to God alone. No human hand or sleight of hand could light this fire.

Read 1 Kings 18:36–39. What is at the heart of Elijah's prayer?

What do the people declare in response to the fiery display?

Elijah executes the wicked prophets of Baal. Hearing the rumbling of a rainstorm, the prophet instructs King Ahab to enjoy a meal. Then Elijah, whose relationship with God is marked by prayer, calls out to God and rain falls, ending the famine. Ahab races to tell Jezebel, but Elijah miraculously beats him there. Jezebel is infuriated that the false prophets have died and puts out a death sentence on Elijah.

Read 1 Kings 19:3–4. What do negative thought spirals cause Elijah to think, do, and say?

What are some of the negative thought spirals you struggle with? Circle any that apply.

I am not enough.

It's just a matter of time until things get worse.

I should be further along by now.

I'm alone in this.

Things will never get better.

I'm unlovable.

People always let me down.

Everyone else has it better.

Other: ________________________________

How does the truth of God's love and acceptance, as well as God's Word, combat these false beliefs?

> Like Elijah, we need proper nourishment and rest. Our spiritual health, physical wellness, and mental health are intertwined.

Even though no one in Scripture performs more miracles than Elijah (other than Jesus), the prophet loses hope. Yet God doesn't leave him there.

Read 1 Kings 19:5–9. How does God meet Elijah in the following areas of need?

- PHYSICALLY:

- EMOTIONALLY:

- SPIRITUALLY:

Then God brings Elijah to a place where they can have an honest conversation and Elijah can encounter and know God in a way he never has before.

Read 1 Kings 19:9–18. Recognizing Elijah's emotional and spiritual state, how does the Lord address the prophet's concerns?

What does this reveal about God's character?

God, in His great love, gives Elijah a companion in ministry known as Elisha. This young man will walk alongside and serve the aged prophet for years to come. Their relationship is one of many throughout Scripture that reminds us we aren't meant to make this journey of faith by ourselves. Whether it's by joining a Bible study or being part of a faithful church body, we are wired to find restoration, encouragement, and support through doing life with other people.

What's one burden you feel like you need to carry alone?

How might sharing that burden with a safe, caring person or group of believers help lighten the load?

Eventually, Elijah's earthly ministry comes to an end, and Elisha takes up his mantle. Elisha asks for a double portion of Elijah's spirit (2 Kings 2:9), and God grants it. In the end, Elijah never really dies.

Read 2 Kings 2:11. How does God meet Elijah at the end of his life?

What does this reveal about Elijah's relationship with God?

Just as Elijah fights feelings of discouragement and isolation, we, too, can believe the lies of the enemy. We can look around and wrongly believe we are the only ones standing in the gap, doing the work God has called us to. But as Elijah's story reminds us, there are thousands of others who have not bowed their knees.

On the continuum below, mark how much you struggle with feeling like you're the only one doing God's work or getting discouraged.

I don't struggle with feeling like I'm the only one doing God's work or get discouraged at all. ○———○———○———○———○———○———○ I struggle with feeling like I'm the only one doing God's work or get discouraged often.

In the space below, write a prayer asking God to help you recognize that you are not alone in whatever you're facing and fill you with courage.

Connect

Now that you've read and reflected on much of Elijah's story, it's time to connect this person of the Bible with your own life. Fill out the chart below.

What does Elijah's story teach you about navigating feelings of discouragement and thinking you're the only one doing God's work?	
What challenges or encourages you most in Elijah's story?	
What does Elijah's story reveal to you about overcoming discouragement?	
How do you hope to walk in greater confidence in God after studying the life of Elijah?	

Reveal

Now that you've connected Elijah's story with your own life, it's time to look at how God reveals His character and faithfulness to Elijah and how God is doing the same for you.

Where do you see God show up in Elijah's life, and what does that reveal about God?	
What does God reveal to you about His character and faithfulness through the life of Elijah?	
What does Elijah's story suggest or reveal about the way God wants to empower you?	

Pray

Take a few minutes to ask the Holy Spirit to guide you as you respond to the following prayer prompts.

Lord, like Elijah, help me . . .

Lord, how is discouragement getting the best of me in this season? What's Your perspective and the truth I most need to hear?

Lord, who is someone I need to reach out to and encourage? What's the best way to do that?

Lord, considering Elijah's story, how are You calling me to live differently?

LESSON ELEVEN

Jesus' Ultimate Overcoming

[Jesus] is the ultimate Overcomer. By crushing sin and death, Jesus gave us eternal life and hope. He was so filled with compassion that He left the glories of heaven to descend to us, knowing the disregard and torture He would suffer before being executed like a common criminal. Who does that?

SHANNON BREAM
from *Nothing Is Impossible with God*

The God of the universe, the One who created you in His own image, loves you more than you know. In fact, He loves you and all of humanity so much that He sent His own Son to become a bridge, taking on every sin that will ever be committed, bearing the weight of everything that separated us from our heavenly Father—all so we can live in a vibrant, holy relationship with God.

No matter what we're facing, the presence of God, through a relationship with Jesus, changes everything. It's His nearness that speaks to our pain. It's His presence that walks us through the deepest of valleys and the darkest of nights. It's His love that binds up our wounds and carries us through. Through Christ, nothing we face is impossible!

Reflect

The presence of God isn't a fuzzy feeling or the absence of trouble but a relationship with a real person. And it's the relationship part that's so important.

Sure, God is always present and always everywhere. But the Bible's idea of living in God's presence is more than physically inhabiting the same space as God.

In the Old Testament, God's glory was everywhere but especially dwelled in the tabernacle (and later the temple in Jerusalem), in a sacred room called the holy of holies, sealed off by a curtain.

Read Exodus 26:31–33. What instructions does God give Moses regarding the construction of the holy of holies?

Only the high priest could enter the holy of holies, and only once a year—on the Day of Atonement (Leviticus 16:34). Throughout the Old Testament, God instructs His people to make various offerings for the forgiveness of sins. These include burnt offerings, grain offerings, guilt offerings, and more.

Read Hebrews 10:1–4, 11. What are animal sacrifices unable to do?

God's redemption plan for the world was to send His own Son, Jesus, to become the ultimate sacrifice. Jesus would accomplish what a grain or bull offering never could.

Read Hebrews 10:8–10, 12–18. How does Jesus' death and resurrection change how forgiveness is given and received?

The redemption God offers comes at an incredible cost. Jesus is beaten, mocked, whipped, publicly humiliated, and nailed to a cross. All for us. All for you.

Read John 3:16 and Romans 8. What motivates God to demonstrate such sacrificial love?

Jesus, resurrected, can be a champion for our cause—
because He isn't just our defender but also our substitute.

Jesus' death on the cross and resurrection puts an end to the separation between people and God. This symbolic reality is demonstrated at Christ's death.

Read Mark 15:37–38. What happens to the curtain in the temple when Jesus takes His last breath on the cross?

Through His sacrificial death, Jesus tears down every barrier. Our debt to the Holy God is paid forever.

Read Hebrews 10:19–22. What does Jesus' victory over sin and death enable us to do?

What joy, what relief, what salvation! Does this mean we'll never sin again? No, but we know that God provides a way through it.

Read 1 Corinthians 10:13. What does God do whenever we face temptation?

Read Romans 6:1–4. What does Christ's death and resurrection empower us to do when it comes to sin?

We must remember that when God looks at us, He doesn't see our sin but the righteousness of Jesus. When God looks at you, He sees Jesus. That means He can have the relationship with us that He has always had with His Son. That's how a holy God can pour out His presence into the hearts of His people. No longer is His glory confined to the holy of holies.

This is great news! But what we can see clearly now was hard to see from inside it.

For centuries, God's prophets had pointed toward the Messiah to come. Most Jews expected the Messiah to have an earthly kingdom through which he would deliver victory to God's people. They couldn't imagine that a humble manual laborer wandering the countryside and telling puzzling stories was God Himself! But there were clues along the way.

Using the passages below, fill in the chart with each Old Testament prophecy and its fulfillment in Jesus in the New Testament.

Prophecy of the Messiah	Fulfillment of Prophecy	Event from Jesus' Life
Isaiah 7:14	*Matthew 1:18, 22–23*	
Micah 5:2	*Matthew 2:1*	
Isaiah 40:3–4	*John 1:23*	
Zechariah 9:9	*Matthew 21:1*	
Zechariah 11:12–13	*Matthew 27:6–10*	
Isaiah 53:3	*John 1:11*	

Despite all the prophecies regarding His life, death, and resurrection, many struggled to recognize Jesus as the Messiah. He readily upended people's expectations and what was culturally conventional. He included women and the marginalized in His ministry. He called out the religious leaders and corrected His own disciples. He was building a different kind of kingdom and almost no one seemed to understand it.

So if you ever feel worried that you just can't understand God's plan, or that you keep misunderstanding it, be comforted. Even Jesus' disciples, who spent every day with Him, couldn't figure it out.

Yet because of who Christ is—Immanuel, God with us—we can find the strength to overcome. The beauty of Christ's being fully God and fully human is that He knows our struggles. He knows the breadth of emotions we face, from overwhelming joy to the crushing depths of sorrow.

Read Hebrews 4:15–16. What comfort do you find in knowing that Jesus has felt pain and offers mercy and grace regardless of what you are going through?

Read 2 Corinthians 1:3–5. Describe a time when the comfort you received from God became a source of comfort you were able to offer to someone else.

With Jesus, nothing is impossible because God is with us! We can turn to Him in prayer with full confidence that He is already praying for us.

Read Hebrews 7:24–25. What encouragement do you find in knowing Jesus lives to intercede for you?

While Jesus' sacrifice doesn't prevent us from going through hard things, it can powerfully comfort us when we know God will be with us through it all. When you make the decision to follow Jesus—which is the best decision you'll ever make—you no longer have to face anything on your own. You're never alone. You can live in the fullness of becoming an overcomer because of all He has conquered on your behalf. Never forget that God is with you and for you, no matter what may come.

On the continuum below, mark how much of your life and heart you're giving fully to Jesus.

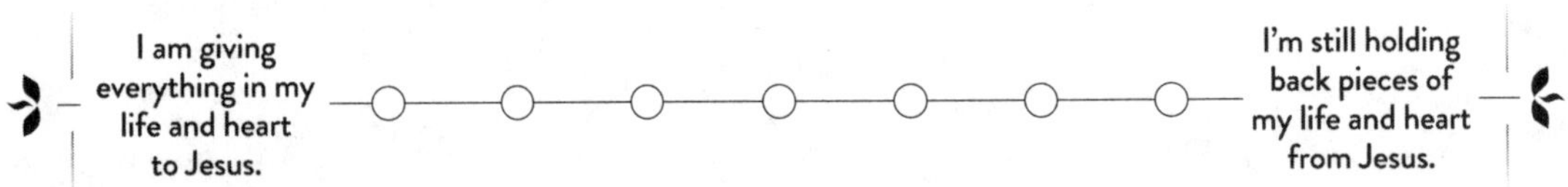

In the space below, write a prayer asking Jesus to come fully into your heart once again and that your whole life can be used to honor and glorify Him.

Connect

Now that you've read and reflected on the life and sacrifice of Christ, it's time to connect Scripture with your own life. Fill out the chart below.

What does Jesus' story teach you about overcoming sin and death?	
What challenges or encourages you most about Jesus' life, death, and resurrection?	
What does Jesus teach you about overcoming impossible situations?	
How do you hope to walk in greater confidence in God after studying how Jesus overcame the world?	

Reveal

Now that you've made connections between Jesus and your own life, it's time to look at how God reveals His character and faithfulness through Jesus.

What was accomplished by God sending His own Son to die for us? What are you still trying to accomplish that Jesus has already done?	
What's your biggest personal takeaway about Jesus through His life, death, and resurrection?	
What steps can you take to nourish a richer, deeper, more intimate relationship with Jesus?	

Pray

Take a few minutes to ask the Holy Spirit to guide you as you respond to the following prayer prompts.

Jesus, You know my deepest struggles more intimately than anyone. Please help me . . .

Jesus, what means of escape have You provided that will allow me to resist temptation in my life? At my job? With my loved ones?

Jesus, You are acquainted with grief, and You know the places in my life where I hurt the most. How can I experience the comfort and peace You provide?

Considering this entire study, how are You calling me to live differently in the impossible situation I face?

ABOUT THE AUTHOR

Shannon Bream

currently serves as anchor of FOX News Sunday. She is author of the number-one *New York Times* bestseller *Women of the Bible Speak*. Shannon also serves as Chief Legal Correspondent for the network and host of the *Livin' the Bream* podcast. She's anchored a wide variety of coverage for high-profile stories including landmark Supreme Court decisions, history-making storms, Capitol Hill scandals, and endless presidential campaigns. She graduated magna cum laude from Liberty University and earned a Juris Doctorate with honors from Florida State University College of Law. Before beginning her journalism career, Shannon worked as an attorney specializing in sexual harassment and race discrimination cases. She's grateful to be a messenger of the greatest story ever told: God loves you and wants a relationship with you. Shannon is happiest at home with her husband, Sheldon; their dog, Biscuit; and a good book!

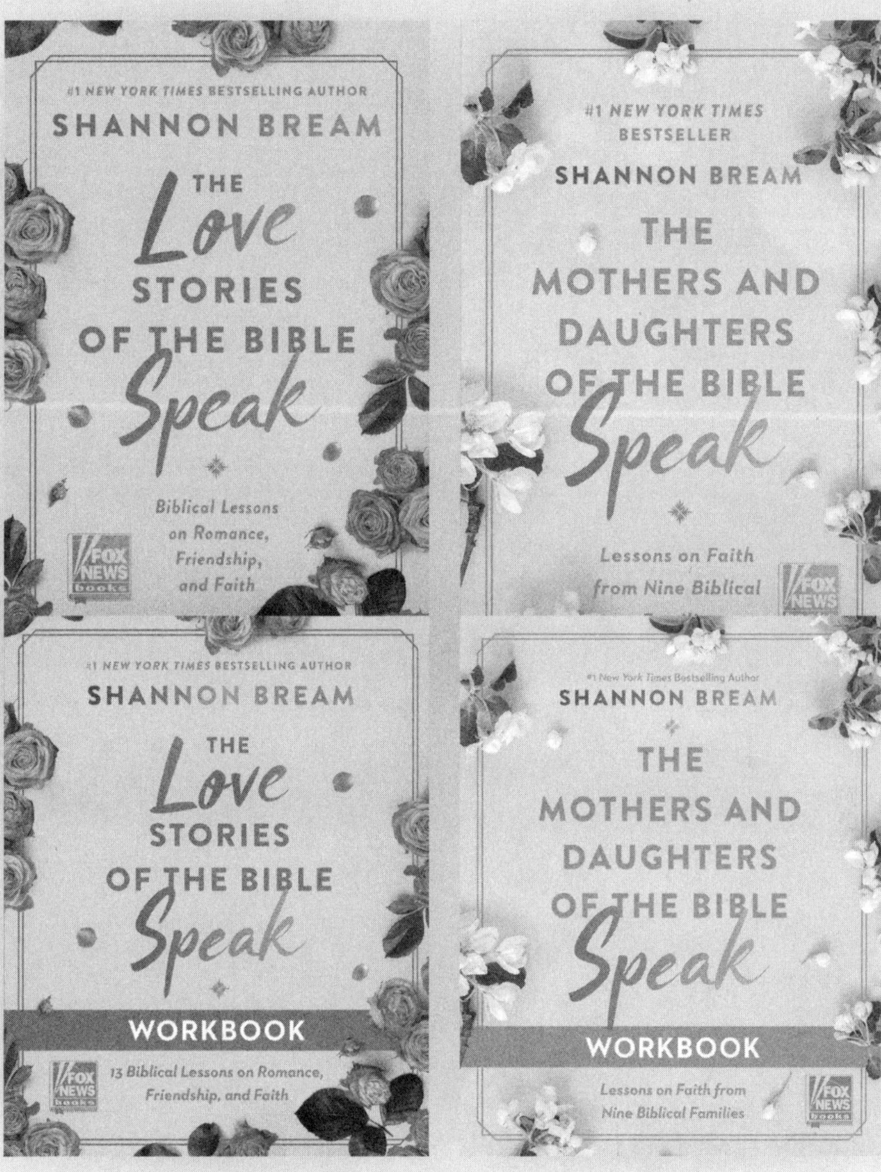
#1 NEW YORK TIMES BESTSELLING AUTHOR
SHANNON BREAM
THE Love STORIES OF THE BIBLE Speak
Biblical Lessons on Romance, Friendship, and Faith
#1 NEW YORK TIMES BESTSELLER
SHANNON BREAM
THE MOTHERS AND DAUGHTERS OF THE BIBLE Speak
Lessons on Faith
from Nine Biblical
#1 NEW YORK TIMES BESTSELLING AUTHOR
SHANNON BREAM
THE Love STORIES OF THE BIBLE Speak
WORKBOOK
13 Biblical Lessons on Romance, Friendship, and Faith
#1 New York Times Bestselling Author
SHANNON BREAM
THE MOTHERS AND DAUGHTERS OF THE BIBLE Speak
WORKBOOK
Lessons on Faith from Nine Biblical Families

From the Publisher

GREAT STUDIES

ARE EVEN BETTER WHEN THEY'RE SHARED!

Help others find this study:

- Post a review at your favorite online bookseller.
- Post a picture on a social media account and share why you enjoyed it.
- Send a note to a friend who would also love it—or, better yet, go through it with them.

Thanks for helping others grow their faith!